The New McG
Reader

William Holmes McGuffey

Alpha Editions

This edition published in 2022

ISBN: 9789356712492

Design and Setting By

Alpha Editions

awww.alphaedis.com

Email - info@alphaedis.com

Contents

PREFACE

The New McGuffey First Reader has been prepared in conformity with the latest and most approved ideas regarding the teaching of reading, and its lessons embody and illustrate the best features of the word, the phonic, and the sentence or thought methods.

While all the stories in this book are new, or have been rewritten especially for its pages, care has been taken to preserve the distinguishing characteristics which have given to the McGuffey Readers their unparalleled popularity and usefulness.

The gradation both in thought and in words has been carefully maintained, and the work provided enables the pupils to advance by easy and evenly progressive stages from the beginning to the end.

Only a few new words are introduced at each lesson, and these are repeated frequently in succeeding lessons until the pupils are able to recognize them without difficulty.

From the first lesson script is presented in connection with the printed forms of words, the frequency of its use diminishing as the printed forms become more familiar.

The sounds of the letters are taught, in the order of the alphabet, by appropriate exercises after the various reading lessons. The phonic elements and the common diacritical marks are learned one at a time and in a manner that is both natural and easy.

A a N n
B b O o
C c P p
D d Q q
E e R r
F f S s
G g T t
H h U u
I i V v
J j W w
K k X x
L l Y y
M m Z z

FIRST READER

---

a boy I see

boy I see a boy

I see a boy

---

girl can and the girl

I see a girl.

I see a boy.

I see a boy and a girl.

The boy can see the girl.

I can see the girl and the boy.

I can see the girl.

---

man has hat run

See the man!

See the boy and the man!

The man has a hat.

Has the boy a hat?

The boy can run.

Can the man run?

The man can see the boy run.

a man can has hat a

---

doll have my

I have a hat.

I have a doll.

See my doll!

Can the doll see?

I can see my doll.

Has the doll a hat?

My doll has a hat.

The girl has a doll and a hat.

a can has hat have a

_____

play may take ball

Can the boy play?

The boy can run and play.

The boy can play ball.

Can the man play ball?

The man may see the boy play.

May the man take the hall?

The boy may take the ball.

a may play take a

_____

baby little big

Can the girl see the baby?

Can the baby see the little girl?

The baby has a big doll.

The little girl has a ball.

I can see the baby.

Can the baby see my big hat?

The baby may have my ball.

Take the ball, baby!

a may play take baby a

_____

dog it he with

The man has a little dog.

The boy has a big dog.

See the little dog run!

He has my ball.

May the big dog have it?

May he take it?

The little dog may have the ball.

He may run and play with it.

b big boy ball baby b

———————————

bird she not fly

See the little bird!

May the baby have it?

May she take it?

She can not take it.

The bird can fly.

The baby can not have the bird.

She can not fly.

She may play with my doll.

She may have my big hat.

b baby big bird b

———————————

cow is good to

I see a man and a dog and a cow.

The cow is with the man.

The dog has a big hat.

He is a good little dog.

He may take the hat to the man.

The man is good to the dog.

The cow can run. She can not play.

c can cow c

_____

catch come you me

The baby can not have the bird.

She can not fly and catch it.

Can she catch the good little girl?

Come, baby, come!

Come and catch me.

Catch me and my big doll.

Catch me, and you may have the doll.

You may have it to play with.

c can catch come c

_____

REVIEW.

The boy has a big dog.

You may see the dog play ball.

Can he catch it?

May I run and take it?

The man with the big hat has a cow.

The girl is good to the little baby.

The baby may have my big doll.

She can not catch the bird.

She may come with me and see the bird fly.

_____

REVIEW.

can man me see

cow come run is

he has have hat

boy ball baby big

dog doll not bird

girl good you my

play may fly to

little catch and it

take she with the

———————————

one two drum go

Come with me, and see the boys.

One little boy has a drum.

Two boys have big hats.

One boy has a ball.

See the boys go!

See the boys go with the drum.

One, two; one, two; drum, drum!

d dog doll drum d

———————————

dress red glad will

The girls have come to play with the baby.

Two girls have little dolls.

One girl has a red dress.

The baby is glad to see the girls.

The girl with the red dress is May.

May is glad to see the good baby.

She will take the baby to see the bird.

d dress red glad bird d

_____

we are three in field

Come with me, little May.

We will go to the field.

We will go and see the cows.

The cows are in the field.

My cow is red.

Two cows are not red.

One and two are three.

We have three cows.

e me we he she e

_____

tree pretty high

Three birds are in the tree.

One is a pretty red bird.

You can not catch it.

It is high in the tree.

The red bird can see the boys with the drum.

It can see the little girl with the red dress.

It can see the good baby and the pretty doll.

It can see the man in the field.

Pretty birds, will you fly to me?

ee see tree three ee

_____

wagon let get ride now

The little boy has a red wagon.

Is it not a pretty one?

The boy will let little May ride in it.

Come, May, come and see my wagon.

You may get in it, and have a ride.

I will take you with me to the fields.

You may have a good ride.

Is the drum in the wagon?

Let me get it. Now we will go.

e red let get e

_____

apple yellow yes too if

See my pretty red apple!

I have three good apples.

One is red, and two are yellow.

I will give you the red one.

May I have a yellow one, too?

Yes. if you are a good girl.

I see a big red apple in the tree.

Will you let me get it?

Yes, you may if it is not too high.

e yes yellow get let red e

_____

Frank flowers find they them

Frank and little May are in the field with the wagon.

They have come to find flowers.

May has a red flower.

Frank has three yellow flowers.

He will let May have them.

She will take them to the wagon

She is glad to get the pretty flowers.

f field kind flowers Frank f

_____

by nest here feed

Come here, girls! I see a nest.

Little birds are in it.

One, two, three.

The little birds can not fly.

They are not pretty.

They will get pretty by and by.

The big bird is not here now.

She is high in the apple tree.

She will come to them by and by.

She will come and feed them.

g girls get glad big g

_____

woods like home horse

The boys like to go to the woods.

Here they are now.

Here are the horse and the wagon.

And here is the boy with the drum.

They like to play in the woods.

They like to find pretty flowers.

If they find little birds in a nest, they will not take them.

By and by they will go home.

They will ride home in the wagon.

h here high home horse h

_____

sit give but whip

Will you let me ride home with you, Frank?

Yes, May, you may sit by me in the wagon if you like.

Get in, and give me the whip.

I will not whip the good horse.

Now, here we go! Here is the apple tree, but we can not see the nest in it.

i sit give is whip think

REVIEW.

Here are three boys and two girls by the big apple tree.

One boy has a yellow drum and one has a whip.

The boy in the red wagon is Frank.

The girls are glad to see Frank.

He will give them a ride.

They like to go with him to the fields and the woods.

May we ride with you, Frank?

Yes, girls, get in! And you, too, boys!

Sit by me and see the good horse go.

Now we will go to the woods to find flowers and see the pretty birds.

In one tree you can see a nest, but you can not see the little birds.

You may see the big bird if she comes to feed the little ones.

She has a pretty home high in the tree.

REVIEW.

we are in now

one red ride sit

drum dress tree two

go give get glad

will let here nest

home horse three them

woods too if they

field find feed flowers

by yes high wagon

like whip but Frank

apple yellow pretty May

―――――――

this do kite father gave

Do you see this? It is my kite.

My father gave it to me.

Is it not a pretty one?

He gave me this drum, too.

You may go with me and see me fly my kite.

You may take the drum with you.

Are you not glad my father gave it to me?

i I like high kite i

―――――――

how far as jump John

Frank and John are in the field.

They have come here to play.

How high can you jump, Frank?

Can you jump as high as this?

I can not jump high, John, but
I can jump far.

See! I can jump as far as to the big apple tree.

Now, John, let me see you jump.

j John jump j

―――――――

does her kitten kind

Here is May with her kitten.

Her mother gave the kitten to her.

She is kind to the pretty kitten.

She likes to see it jump and play.

See it run with May's ball!

It does not run far with it.

If May can get the ball she will not take it.

She will give it to the kitten to play with.

k kitten kind like take can c

---

all love away Lucy him fast

This is little Lucy.

Her home is far away.

She has come to see Frank and May.

All the little girls love Lucy.

They are kind and good to her, and she loves them.

Frank will let her ride with him in the big wagon.

He will give her the whip, and the horse will go fast.

The horse will go fast and far, but he will not run away.

l let little love all will l

---

keep think morning look many

Look, Frank! See my pretty flowers.

Mother gave them to me.

She gave them to me this morning.

Do you not think they are pretty?

How many flowers have I?

Here are three my mother gave me.

My father gave me two red ones.

How many are three and two?

I will keep the red flower.

I will give all my yellow flowers to Lucy. She will like them.

She will take them home with her.

m man many mother me

———————————

must your four at

Good morning, little bird.

Good morning, kind Lucy.

How pretty your nest is, little bird!

May I look at the little ones in it?

Yes, you may look at them, but you must not take them away.

How many birds have you?

Let me see. One, two, three, four.

I do not think they are pretty.

They may not be pretty now, but I love them, little girl.

n nest not in many n

———————————

gone on very his

Frank has gone to the field with his kite. He likes to play with it.

It is the kite his father gave him.

He will run and the kite will fly.

He can run very fast, and the kite can fly very high.

John does not like to run with a kite.

He likes to play on his drum.

He will play on his drum, and
Frank will run with his kite.

o on gone John dog o

———————————

oh of rose some

Oh, mother, come here!

See this pretty flower.

I think it is a rose.

Is it not a yellow rose?

Yes, May. It is a yellow rose.

If you will come with me,

I will give you some red roses.

May I have them to keep, mother?

You may keep some of them, but you must give some to Lucy.

Oh, yes! I will give her four red roses, and one yellow rose.

I will give her some to take home to her mother, too.

Do you like yellow roses, mother?

Yes, May, I think they are very pretty.

o oh rose home four o

BOOK SAID CARE WAS

John was a good boy this morning.

His mother gave him a pretty book.

He was very glad.

"Oh, mother," he said, "how kind you are to give me this book!

I think it is very pretty."

"You must take good care of it," said his mother.

"Yes, mother," said John, "and I will let Lucy and May look at it too.

They like to look at pretty books."

"The girls will think you are a very kind little boy.

They will take good care of your book."

oo book look good oo

---

school soon going new other

All the boys and girls are going to school this morning.

You can see them as they go.

Little Lucy is not with them.

She has gone to her home, far away.

But I see May and some other girls.

John has his new book. Some of the other boys have books, too.

I do not see Frank, but I think he will come soon.

oo too school soon do to o

_____

found pet took after picture

Look at this picture.

It is the picture of my pet kitten.

Do you not think she is a pretty pet?

One morning as I was going to school, I found this kitten.

She was by a tree in the woods.

After school I took her home.

"Mother," I said, "see this pretty little kitten. May I keep her as a pet?"

Mother said, "You may keep her if you will take good care of her."

I am kind to my kitten.

I feed her and she loves me.

p pet picture pretty keep p

_____

REVIEW.

My mother gave me a new book.

I took it to school one morning, to let the girls see the pictures.

Soon after this I found my pet kitten and took her home with me.

I like to play with my pet kitten.

I will do as mother says. I will take good care of the kitten.

I love little Lucy. But now she has gone far away to her home.

I like to see John run with his kite.

He can run as fast as the other boys, but he can not jump far.

He does not like to look at books and pictures, but he can play on a drum.

[missing text on page 42]

REVIEW.

as on soon rose must was now some care at do said her him his how oh all love but keep kite kitten kind look book took does think pet picture other mother father far fast four found after of away many very Lucy John morning gone going your school gave jump this

---

goes read tell write well name

The name of this little girl is Rose.

Do you think she looks like a rose?

Do you think Rose is a pretty name?

Rose goes to school.

She can read and write.

At home, she likes to read to her mother. She likes to look at the pictures, too.

Tell me, Rose, how well you can read.

Can you read well in your book?

I think you can write very well.

Can you write your name?

r rose read run her your r

---

were so day then be

Can you tell me the name of this pretty little bird?

It is so little it can not fly very far.

Some of the boys found it in the woods, as they were going to school one day.

It was not in a nest.

Frank said; "I will take the little bird home with me.

It will be a good pet."

So Frank took it as he said.

He is kind to it and feeds it. but he will not keep it.

Some day it can fly well.

Then Frank will let it go.

It will fly away with the other birds.

s so some said nice c

---

us our shall learn children their

Come, girls let us play with our dolls.

We will play school.

Our dolls will be the children.

Our dolls are as good as some children are.

They have their books, and I think, they will learn very fast.

Soon we shall see how well they can read.

This doll is not so good as the others.

She does not like to go to school very well.

She must sit by me and look at her book.

As soon as she can read well, she may go home and play.

She goes to school day after day, but she does not learn.

She can not write at all.

She can not tell her name.

WRITING LESSON.

This is my little doll.

Her name is Lucy.

Do you thik she is pretty?

s as dolls does goes is

---

tall Henry am table what

"How tall you are, Henry!"

"Yes, father, I shall soon be a man.
I am as tall as the table, now."

"What can you see on the table?"

"I can see your big book, father."

"What do you see by the book?"

"Oh, I see some pictures. Two pictures are by the book, and two are not
by the book."

"How many are two and two, Henry?"

"Two and two are four."

"You do well. If you learn fast, you may soon go to school.

Then you can learn how to read and write."

t tall table tell what not t

---

funny pail up hill water there

Oh, mother, come and look at this funny picture.

What do you see in the picture Lucy?

I see two children in the picture.

I see a tall boy and little girl.

How fast they run!

They are going up hill, too.

The boy has a pail.

I think he is going to get a pail of water for his mother.

How very funny it must be to run up hill!

Will they find water on the hill?

Oh, yes, I see a well up there.

They must be good children to go so far after a pail of water.

There must be good water in the well.

  Jack and Jill went up the hill,
 To get a pail of water;
Jack fell down and broke his crown,
 And Jill came tumbling after.

u up run must funny u

_____

says say out sure June

Our mother says we may go and see little Lucy.

We are going some day in June, soon after our school is out.

We do not have school in June.

Lucy's home is far away.

We shall ride there in the big wagon with father and mother.

Father says it will take all day to go so far.

Mother says I must be sure to take
Lucy some of our good apples.

I will take her a book, too.

I am sure Lucy will be glad to see us. She will run out to the wagon and
tell us so.

What do you think she will say?

She will say, "Oh, May, I am so glad you have come."

u sure June Lucy u

_____

violets sweet buy who

  Violets sweet, violets sweet!
Who will buy my violets sweet?
Violets sweet, violets sweet!
I will buy your violets sweet.

_____

vine bush wild grow

See this funny little tree!

What kind of tree is it?

It is not a tree, it is a vine.

It is not so tall as some trees.

It looks like a wild rose vine.

Will it have roses on it?

Yes, I think some roses will grow on it; but I am not sure.

Wild roses come in June.

Some of them are very sweet.

My roses are not wild.

They do not grow on a vine.

They grow on a bush.

A bush looks like a little tree.

v vine very have give v

---

went came would down street sell

Little Henry went to school this morning.

All the children were glad to see him as he came down the street.

He is a funny little boy, and I am sure you would like him.

He says he will grow very fast and soon be a man.

He likes to go to school.

REVIEW.

One day Henry took a pail with him and went up the hill.

Do you think he went to get a pail of water? I do not think so.

He went to find violets and wild flowers in the woods.

After a little he came down; but he would not let me look in his pail.

He would not tell me how many flowers were in it.

"Who will buy my wild roses?" he said. "Who will buy my sweet violets?

I came down the street to sell my flowers. But now I must say they do not sell very well."

w went well wild would way w

---

sun sunflower know

Do you know the name of this big yellow flower?

What kind of flower is it?

Oh, I know.

It is a sunflower.

Does it look like the sun?

It likes the sun.

Do you know what sunflowers are good for?

Yes, they are good to look at.

If you will go to the field on the hill, you may see many of them.

They are not sweet flowers, like your violets and some others.

If you will give me one of your pretty roses, you may have all the sunflowers I can find.]

I like roses and sweet violets.

I like to see big, yellow sunflowers, too; but I do not care to take them home with me. Do you?

y you yes yellow y

---

try from for about

Come here, Henry, and sit by me at the table.

Your mother has gone out to buy a new book for you.

She says you must learn to read.

I am sure you will try to learn.

Then you can read about the pretty birds, and the tall sunflowers, and good children at school.

Soon you may take your book to school.

See this picture, Henry.

It is a picture of a little bird.

I think it is a yellow bird.

The bird has a pretty nest in the woods.

Would you not like to see the little ones in it?

By and by, they will come out and try to fly.

Very soon you may see them as they fly from bush to bush.

y by try fly my buy y

WRITING LESSON.

I have a book.
I learn to read in it.
I can write my name.

---

bee busy buzz sing work

We fly about from flower to flower.

We sing as we work.

Would you like to know what we sing?

We sing, "Buzz, buzz."

You will say,
    "What a funny way to sing!"

But we do not care what you say.

We are too busy to think about it.

You must not keep us from our work.

What is as busy as a bee?

All day it sings as it works,
    "Buzz, buzz, buzz!"

How doth the little busy bee
Improve each shining hour?
It gathers honey all the day
From every bud and flower.

s bees buzz busy z

A B C SONG. [musical notation omitted]

A B C D E F G
H I J K L M N O P
Q R S T U V W
Q R S T U V W
X... Y... Z, O dear me!
I can not say my A B C.

---

when warm walk these

One morning when the sun was warm these children went out to take a walk.

Do you know who they are?

I see May and Rose and little Lucy.

There are two other girls with them, but I do not know their names.

They took a little wagon with them, and went up the hill.

They went to the field on the hill to find some violets.

They found some sunflowers in the field, but violets do not grow there.

They saw a wild rose, but a busy bee was on it.

"Now," said Lucy, "let us go to the well and see if it has water in it."

"Yes," said one of the other girls, "the sun is too hot here. But if we go to the well, you must take care not to fall in."

"Oh, I will not fall in," said Lucy.

"I will look at the water far down in the well; but I will not fall."

The girls will go home when the sun goes down.

a warm walk water fall a

---

star garden sky time could

I see you, little star.

Do you see me?

I am in the garden.

My name is Lucy.

I see you far up in the sky.

How very high you are!

If you will look down, you can see me.

You can see the flowers, too.

If you would come in the day time, you could see all the children.

You could see us going to school.

But it is time for me to go in now.

Take care, little star, and do not fall

a star far garden are a

---

green that shade thank plant

[Missing part of page 65]

They grow in the shade.

Rose found three little yellow flowers.

They are not so pretty as the violets.

"I think that all wild flowers are pretty," said Rose.

"Well, then'" said Frank, "you may have these violets that I found.

In June I will find you some roses."

[Missing part of page 66]

---

been help done corn behind

These boys have been in the field all the morning.

What do you think they do in the field?

They do not go out there to play.

They go to the field to work.

They help their father plant corn.

They are now on their way home.

One of the boys rides on the horse.

The other two walk behind.

Do you think that these boys like to work?

They will like to play when their work is done.

Do you know what corn is?

Would you like to see how it grows in the field?

This is the way it looks.

It is very green and pretty.

It grows to be as tall as a tall man.

Do you know what corn is good for?

th these they there their father

---

much went each cents more to-day

Would you like to buy some apples to-day? I have some very good ones here.

How much do you want for your apples, Frank?

I will sell you the green ones for three cents each. But I must have more for these yellow ones. They are sweet apples.

I think I must have four cents each for these.

Oh, Frank! You want too much for your apples. We can not buy them to-day. We can not give so much.

Well, then, children, I will tell you what I will do. I will give you as many apples as you want.

Thank you, Frank. You are very kind. Will you give one of your sweet apples to each of us?

Yes, here are three apples for each of you; and I have four to take home to mother.

Can you tell how many apples Frank has?

Is he not a good, kind boy to give all his apples away?

ch each much children ch

---

where way which why or

Come, Henry, let us take a walk this warm morning. Where would you like to go?

Shall we go to the green woods?

Or shall we go down to the field and help the boys plant corn?

Tell me which way we shall go.

Oh, let us go out where the wild flowers grow.

Then we can see the birds in the trees, and the bees at their work.

Why do the bees fly from flower to flower? Do they like to work when the sun is warm?

Tell me why the bees are so busy all the day.

I will tell you all about them when we have found one at work. But come now, let us walk out to the green woods.

wh when where which why wh

---

set shines moon bright light night

These four children have gone out to see the sun set.

The sun is high in the sky now.

By and by it will set behind the hills.

The sun shines in the day time.

It helps to keep us warm.

It gives us light.

When it goes down we have night.

Then the stars come out and shine.

The moon shines at night, too.

But it is not so bright as the sun.

On some nights the moon does not shine at all.

Do you like to see the moon?

Yes, I like to see it.

I like to see its pretty light.

We can look at the moon; but we can not look at the sun.

It is too bright for us to look at.

ight night bright light ight

---

leaves should ripe eat wish

Let us sit here in the shade under our old apple tree.

You can look up and see the green leaves and the little green apples.

I should like to have one of the apples. I wish you would get it for me, Frank.

Why do you want it? It is not ripe.

All the apples on the tree are green, and you must not eat them.

Do you see how little they are?

But the bright sun will shine on them day after day.

They will grow and grow; and after a time they will be ripe, and yellow, and good to eat.

Then we will come and sit here in the shade, and you may have as many apples as you can eat.

sh shine shade should wish sh

This is what Henry can write:

My name is Henry.
My name is Henry.

Can you write your name?

---

listen hear wonder honey shut into

Come here, Lucy, and listen. What do you hear in this flower?

Oh, mother! I hear a bee. It goes buzz, buzz, buzz! I wonder how it came to be shut up in the flower?

It went into the flower for some honey, and then the flower shut it in.

Shall we let it out, Lucy?

Oh yes, mother; then it can go to the other flowers and get honey.

o some other wonder honey does o

Robin Redbreast Pussy Cat sat ran

Little Robin Redbreast sat on a tree, Up went Pussy Cat, down went he; Down came Pussy Cat, away Robin ran; Said little Robin Redbreast, "Catch me if you can!"

---

river fish line hook near

One warm day in June, Frank's father said to him: "Frank, I think I will go down to the river and catch some fish."

"Oh, father," said Frank, "I wish I could go too. Will you let me go and help you?"

"Yes, Frank. Run and; get your hook and line."

"Thank you, father, I am so glad that I may go."

Here is Frank at the river, with his hook and line.

How bright the sun shines on the water!

I wonder where all the fish have gone. Frank can not see them.

The fish are far down in the water.

Frank has let his hook down, and he wishes that a big fish would come and take it.

But the fish do not wish him to catch them to-day. They will not come near the hook.

---

blue place above among any saying

What a bright day this is!

The sky is as blue as it can be.

Lucy and her mother are in the woods.

They have found a good place under a green tree.

They sit in the shade of the tree and listen to the birds that are singing above them.

Robin Redbreast is in the tree.

Lucy sees him as he jumps about among the leaves.

By and by he will fly away to his nest.

Lucy wonders where it is.

---

boat oar row deep sometimes road house

John has a new boat.

His father gave it to him.

It is blue, with a bright red line near the water.

He keeps it in the river, not far from the road.

He has some good oars, too.

He keeps the oars at the house.

His home is near the river.

He likes to row up and down the river in his boat.

Sometimes little May goes out in the boat with him.

The water is not deep, and the children will not fall out of the boat. They like to row here and there on the river.

John takes the oars, and May sits in her place and tells him where to go.

Sometimes each takes an oar. Then the boat goes very fast.

John has a hook and line. But when May is with him he does not try to catch any fish.

Shall I tell you why?

He knows that May does not like to see a fish on a hook.

oa oars boat road oa

REVIEW.

Here are all the boys coming up the road. I wonder where they are going to-day.

Each boy has a hook and a line, and one has some light oars.

I think they are going to get into John's new boat and row out on the river.

Can you tell which of these boys is John?

They will get in the boat and row far out on the water.

When they get to a deep place they will try to catch some fish.

I wonder if any of the fish will come near the boat.

————————————

Little Robin Redbreast has a nest in our garden.

If you listen any time in the day, you can hear him sing.

On warm days he likes to sit in the shade among the green leaves.

He can see the busy bees when they fly to the flowers to get honey.

He sees the green apples about him, but he does not like them. He would not eat them if they were ripe and sweet.

At night he can look up from his place in the tree and see the bright stars in the sky. Some times he can see the moon, too, as it shines above him.

Sometimes the Pussy Cat comes under his tree and looks up at him; but she can not get him.

She sits under the tree and wishes that she could catch him.

Do you know why she wants the bird? Do you know what she would do if she could get him?

————————————

One day Henry went out to the field behind the garden. He went out to see his father plant corn.

He sat down by a tree and said,
"Father, shall I help you work?
I have been in the house all day."

"Thank you, my little boy," said his father. "I want some help very much. What can you do?"

"I should like to plant some corn.
How much will you give me?"

"I will give you four cents a day if you work well. But now the sun is about to set, and we must go home."

---

saw made yet float put sail

"What is that?" said Rose as she went down the garden walk.

She saw Frank at work under the apple tree.

"It is a little boat, Rose," said Frank. "What do you think of this boat?"

"Oh, I think it is very pretty. Where did you get it, Frank?"

"I made it, Rose. I made it all."

"How glad I am that you made it! Will it float in the water?"

"I think so. All it wants now is the sail. I will soon put that on."

"How I should like to see it sail! Does mother know that you have made it?"

"Not yet; but I will take it to her as soon as I have put the sail on it.

Then, if she will let us, we will take it down to the river. We will put it in the water and see it float. We will see how fast it can sail."

Soon Frank and Rose were on their way to the river. Frank said that if the boat sailed well, he would give it to Rose.

She will let her doll sail in it.

e her were under river water er _____

wind blow feel face

"Listen, mother, do you hear that?"

"Yes, Henry, it is the wind.

We can hear it blow about the house; but we can not see it.

If you should go out of the house, you could feel it blow in your face."

"See how it blows the leaves about! How fast Frank's little boat would sail with this wind!"

ou out about house how ow

---

summer bloom soft make

Do you know when summer comes?

When summer comes the days are warm and bright.

Green leaves are on the trees.

Flowers bloom in the woods and in the gardens.

The wind blows soft; the sky is blue; the sun shines bright

In the summer the corn grows tall and green. It is then that the children play in the woods.

I like the summer time very much.

———————————

wake sleep long meadow

I wish my baby doll would wake.

Wake up, baby! Wake up!

Do not sleep so long.

It is morning, and all good little dolls should be up.

Oh, baby, what a care you are!

Will you not wake up?

I do not know of any doll that sleeps so long as you do.

Now jump up, and see what a bright morning it is. See how the sun shines. Wake up, baby!

Do you wish to know where I have been, baby doll? I have been down in the meadow with Frank and Rose.

Shall I tell you what we saw?

Well, we saw birds and bees and green leaves and pretty flowers.

Then we went to the river and saw Frank's little boat sail on the water.

a care where there e

———————————

sheep asleep horn no cry

Little Boy Blue,
Come blow your horn.
The sheep's in the meadow,
The cow's in the corn!
Where is the little boy

That looks after the sheep?
Oh, here he is!
Here he is, fast asleep!
Will you wake him? No, not I;
For if I do, I know he will cry.

[Caption to illustration of children playing with beetles.]
Fly away, little bird, fly away home!
If you are not a little bird, why did you come?

---

cold turn begin brown over gold

What will come when summer is over and gone?

Oh, I can tell you. After the summer is gone, fall will come.

When fall comes, the days begin to grow cold.

Then the leaves fall from the trees.

Some of the leaves turn red, some turn brown, and some turn yellow as gold.

In the fall we have ripe apples to eat. The corn is ripe then, too.

All the children are glad when fall comes. Do you know why?

Play time is over, and school begins.

---

rain stay grass fresh

"I wish, mother, you would tell me where the rain comes from.

"Does it come from the sky?

"Are the leaves and the flowers and the grass glad when the rain falls on them?"

This is what Lucy asked her mother one day. Her mother said:

"The rain makes the grass look green and fresh. It helps the flowers grow.

"The corn which we plant in the field could not grow if there was no rain."

"But, mother," said Lucy, "I do not like the rain very well. It makes me stay in the house when I want to go and play.

See how fast it rains! I shall have to stay at home all day."

evening west clouds those fade

It is evening, and the sun is about to set. The day will soon be gone.

Let us sit here on the soft grass and look at the bright clouds in the west.

Do you think there is any rain in those little clouds?

Oh, no! Those are not rain clouds.

See how pretty they are!

Some of the clouds are red, and some are as yellow as gold.

It is the light of the sun that makes them look so bright.

Soon they will all fade away in the blue sky.

Soon it will be night, and the moon and stars will shine for us.

a fast ask grass a

---

ship sea beach sand live shells

Here are four little girls who live near the sea.

They have gone down to the beach with their father.

They like to play in the sand.

Sometimes their mother goes with them, and they stay there all day.

They like to look at the ships as they sail far away on the blue sea.

Do you think you would like to sail far away on a ship?

Sometimes these little girls find pretty shells in the sand.

I think all children like to play on the beach when the sun is warm, and the wind does not blow.

---

only every use driver

What does the man say?

He says, "Good sweet apples, only two cents each! Ripe, sweet apples, yellow as gold! Who will buy my apples this warm summer morning?"

You can hear him as he goes down the road. "Who wants to buy a nice red apple?"

The apples are in the wagon.

The man walks in the road, behind the wagon, and tells every one that he has apples to sell.

His little dog rides in the wagon and looks at the horse.

Is he not a funny driver?

The horse does not go very fast.

He knows that his driver can not use a whip..

"Oh, who wants to buy some good apples this bright summer morning?"

---

just hand told town brother

Do you know these three boys?

The tall boy in the wagon is Frank Brown. The little boy is Henry. He is Frank's brother.

The boy on the horse is John Day. See how well he can ride!

Frank is a good driver. He sits in the wagon, and the horse goes just as he is told.

Frank has a whip in his hand, but he does not use it.

Henry's little dog runs behind. Sometimes he has to run very fast to keep up with the wagon.

Do you know where the boys are going?

I think they are going to town.

I wonder what they will buy in town.

Henry says he will buy a book with pretty pictures in it. He can not read very well, but he likes to look at books.

John wants to ride down to the river and look at the boats. He would buy a new boat if he could. But he has only one cent, and what can he buy with that?

Frank says they will not stay in town long. They must go home very soon.

{Missing pages 103 and 104]

happy often ask bow arrow Robert

The name of this little boy is
Robert. He is a busy boy.

He lives in a big town, and he does not often see the fields and the green woods.

Yet he is just as happy as Frank and John and little Henry.

He lives in a tall house not far from the river. In the summer time he can see the ships as they sail up the river.

His father has a boat, and sometimes
Robert goes sailing in it.

One day Robert saw a man with
[Missing text] bows and arrows to sell.

"How much do you ask for your arrows?" he said.

"[Missing text] three cents each," said the man. "Would you like to buy one?"

Robert did not buy an arrow. He went home and made one that was just as good.

Do you think he can use it?

{Missing text] teacher says that he must
{Missing text] bow now.

What does the summer bring? Green leaves, pretty flowers, busy bees, and birds of many kinds. It is then that we play in the woods and by the sea.

---

winter north ice snow brings short shiver

When winter comes, the days are short and the nights are long.

Then the cold north wind blows over the fields and woods.

It blows over the meadow and the river and the high hills.

It brings snow and ice.

It makes our hands and faces cold. We do not like the north wind.

All children are happy when winter comes. They like to see the snow. They like to play on the ice.

They do not care if the north wind does make them shiver. Those who are dressed warm do not feel the cold very much.

Sometimes the snow is so deep they can not go to school.

In the evening, they sit in the warm house and read and play.

---

room window white story show

It is very cold to day, but the snow is not deep. All the boys and girls are at school.

The school room is warm and bright, and the children are happy.

You can see them at their places in the school room.

They look out of the window and see the snow falling. How soft and white it is!

The teacher has been showing the children some pictures in her new book. Now she is telling them a story that is found in it.

The children look and listen. They do not think how cold it is out of doors.

go ing com ing sing ing -ing fall ing tell ing show ing -ing

---

clock minute call things hour round tick tack

Can you tell what time it is? Look at the clock, and then tell me.

The clock has a round face.

It has two hands.

We call the long hand the minute hand, for it tells the minutes.

We call the short hand the hour hand, for it tells the hours.

How many hours are there in a day? How many minutes in an hour?

If you listen, you can hear what the clock says. Tick, tack, tick, tack.

Our clock at school tells us many things. It tells us when to work and when to play.

SONG OF THE CLOCK.
[Musical notation omitted.]

Tick, tack, tick, tack, tick, tack, tick, tack, Little clock saves me all care. Tick, tack, tick, tack, tick, tack, tick, tack, Tells me when the right hours are, For eating, for sleeping, for play and all, For rising and bathing, it sounds the call; Beat by beat with forward, back, Ever tick and ever tack.

———————

REVIEW.

ship brown made sand meadow sheep brother make soft window shells brings wake sail minute shall bloom fade wind winter should blow face wake summer shade horn stay wish teacher those short steep white sister these north asleep each brother things hour feel obey every

———————

TO BE MEMORIZED.

Children who may read my lay,
This much I have to say;
Each day and every day
Do what is right.
Right things in great or small;
Then, though the sky should fall,
Sun, moon, and stars and all,
You shall have light.

Lightning Source UK Ltd.
Milton Keynes UK
UKHW010647291222
414571UK00004B/170

9 789356 712492